M

A Beginners Guide on How to

Grow Marijuana

Nancy Ross

Table of Contents

Table of Contents
Introduction
Chapter 1: What is Cannabis?
  Benefits of Growing Your Own Cannabis
Chapter 2: Indoor vs. Outdoor Growing
  Indoor Gardening
  Outdoor Gardening
Chapter 3: The Basics of Growing Cannabis
  Steps to Growing Cannabis
  Simple Tools Needed to Grow Cannabis
Chapter 4: Dealing with Pests and Other Gardening Issues
  Best Control Methods for Pests
Chapter 5: Consider a Hydroponic System
  What is Hydroponics?
  Advantages of Hydroponics
  Disadvantages of a Hydroponics System
  Types of Hydroponic Systems
Chapter 6: Troubleshooting Issues With Your Cannabis
  Seeds
  Roots
  Stems
  Leaves
  Flowers
  Harvested Flowers
Conclusion

Introduction

Growing cannabis can be an exciting and fun process. You will get the benefits of growing something that you enjoy using for getting that great high without having to worry about finding the right strain or the cost of getting your cannabis from another source. Many people are interested in growing their own cannabis, but worry about how to even get started. This guidebook is going to help give you the information that you need to start growing cannabis so you can have the best crop possible without all the hassle.

In this guidebook, we will start out with the basics of cannabis including the different names, some of the benefits of using the plant, and so much more. After this, the guidebook is going to take some time to explain the best places to grow your cannabis, how to provide the plant with the right nutrients, and even some of the most common issues that you may encounter including growing issues with the plants and even pests that can pose issues.

Getting started on your cannabis plants can be a big challenge, but once you get some of the basics and get started, you will find that it doesn't have to be too difficult to handle. The cannabis plant can be similar to many of the other plants in your garden in terms of needing the right nutrition, plenty of sunlight, and some water to help them grow big and strong. While there are a few other steps involved with preparing the cannabis to be smoked, a little bit of a green thumb can help you to get started with this exciting adventure as well.

When you are ready to get started with growing your own cannabis plants to get all the benefits that come with having your own plants, make sure to read through this guidebook. It will give you all the facts that you need to ensure that you are growing the best harvest of cannabis possible from the beginning.

Chapter 1: What is Cannabis?

Marijuana is a plant that many people have heard about. Even if you have never used marijuana in the past, you have heard about the various effects it can have on the body, that this plant has become legal in several states in the United States, and that it can even be effective as a treatment for some illnesses. There is still a lot that people do not understand when it comes to this plant. Before you get started with growing cannabis in your home, here is some information to help you understand this plant a bit better.

Cannabis is a plant that often grows wile in temperate and tropical areas of the world, although it is possible to grow this plant in any temperature so don't worry about where you live. The main ingredient that is inside of cannabis is the delta-9 tetrahydrocannabinol, or THC. This is the chemical that is going to give people a high when used as a drug. Of course, there can be a big range of the potency of the THC based on which cannabis product you choose.

There are three main forms of cannabis which are used including hash oil, hashish, and marijuana. Marijuana is basically made from using the dried leaves and flowers of the cannabis plant and it is often the least potent out of the three varieties. Most of the time, people who use marijuana will do so as an edible product or smoke it. Hashish is another form of cannabis that is made using the resin of the plant. This option is dried and then pressed into small blocks before the user smokes it. In some cases, this can also be placed into food and eaten, but this is less common.

The most potent cannabis product is hash oil. This part is made from a thick oil that comes out of the hashish and again is smoked to get the high. No matter which product of cannabis you are using, it is most common to roll up the product as a cigarette, or joint, and then smoke the product to get the high.

Cannabis is illegal in most of the United States, although there are several in the nation that allow the use of cannabis, making it the most widely used illicit drug in the country. The 2012 National

Survey on Drug Use and Health reported that within the past 30 days, about 7.3 percent of people over 12 years old have used marijuana with the average age of using this drug at 17.9. This number has stayed pretty stable for youth over the years but it is expected to grow for other age groups as more states start to allow this drug for purchase.

Cannabis is known under many names, which can make it difficult to track. Some of the other names of cannabis include cones, reefers, brew, joints, hash, weed, Mary Jane, grass, and marijuana.

Many of those who use cannabis, outside of those who are trying it for the first time just to see what it is like, will use this plant in order to experience a sense of relaxation and mild euphoria. This is often known as a high and is something that users enjoy experiencing, especially after a stressful time or suffering from anxiety. The cannabis can change the mood of the user and even changes the way that they perceive and think about the environment around them. This can be a welcome relief to those who are upset about events in their lives or who feel shy and maybe want to get out of their shell.

There are a number of short term effects that can arise from using cannabis. These include:

- Dryness of the throat, mouth, and eyes
- Loss of coordination
- Increased appetite
- Decreased nausea
- Loss of inhibitions
- Drowsiness
- Talkativeness
- Feeling of well-being.

To many people, these benefits can help them to live a more normal life. They may be anxious about all the things that are going on around them or don't have the ability to let loose and have fun. The cannabis may give them this change in perception, perhaps an ability to relax a bit or to not be as worried about embarrassment when out with friends. This high can draw the user back over and over again, allowing them to see the world differently and to feel so much better.

With all its names, the changes that have occurred over the years, and the many people who have given cannabis a try, it is no wonder that many are interested in growing this plant in their own backyards.

Benefits of Growing Your Own Cannabis

Many people have considered growing their own cannabis at home. There are many benefits to doing this. Perhaps you have not been able to get the strain that you want on a regular basis or you want to try out something new. Perhaps you are tired of worrying about getting the right strain or a quality strain that will help you get the right high without all the issues. Purchasing cannabis plants from others can often get expensive compared to just growing them on your own.

While it is a personal choice to grow your own marijuana, it can be a really rewarding experience when you learn how to do it right. Here are some of the best benefits that you can get when you choose to grow your own cannabis.

- Get the strain that you want—sometimes it is hard to get the exact strain that you want. Your seller may not have the right one on hand or you can't find someone who has the one that you would like. Growing your own cannabis plants takes all this hassle out of the process. You can grow the exact strain that you want, regardless of where you live or if others are doing so, and get the exact product that you want.
- Quality control—one of the biggest worries that come from purchasing cannabis is whether the quality is good. Your dealer may promise a good quality, but you have no idea of testing the plant and knowing how good it is until you have already smoked it. Some less reputable sellers may not take as good of care of the plant and you could get sick. But when you grow your own plants, this is no longer a worry. You can watch it through the whole process and ensure that you are

getting a substance that is of the highest quality each and every time.

- Cheaper—it is way cheaper to grow your own cannabis compared to buying it from someone else. When you make a purchase from another person, you are stuck with their prices and their quantity regardless of what you can afford or what you want. But when you grow the plants on your own, you simply need to purchase the seeds, perhaps a few lights if growing inside, and the system you would like to grow with. This can cost a bit when getting started, but the more you use it, the costs go way down.
- Create your own strain—as a beginner, you will probably just want to start out with one strain that you like quite a bit and get used to the whole process. But over time, cross pollination can be an added bonus of the cannabis growing process. You can mix together some different strains and get the one that works out best for you. It can produce the high that you want, or even the taste, much better than from what you get from someone else.

- Get the amount that you want—when you grow your own cannabis, you will be able to choose how much you would like at once. You won't have to worry about being able to get enough from your dealer or someone else. You can grow the exact amount of plants that works for your needs and even keep a little bit extra on hand. This can save some hassle and ensures that you can have cannabis whenever you would like.

So when you are ready to start getting all of these fantastic benefits, read through the rest of this guidebook and learn all of the tips and tricks that you need to know to get the best harvest each and every time.

Chapter 2: Indoor vs. Outdoor Growing

Before you are able to get started on growing your cannabis plants, you need to take care to pick out the right spot. The first question is whether to grow your plants indoors or outdoors. Each of these options has its advantages and disadvantages, and often it is going to be based on the amount of space that you have available and the kind of commitment you would like to make. Let's take a look at some of the benefits of each type of gardening so you can make the right choice for you.

Indoor Gardening

One of the first options you can pick is to grow your cannabis plants indoors. This can be a good option if you are low on outdoor space or you would like to keep an eye on the plants at all times. Here are some things to consider when starting your cannabis plants inside.

Can grow any time of year

Unless you live in an area that is sunny and warm all of the time, there is a substantial part of the year when you can't grow because of the weather. Indoor gardening can take care of this problem. With the right equipment, you will be able to grow your cannabis any time of the year, without worrying about the weather getting too cold, or not enough rain, or one of the other issues that comes with growing outside.

Can pick your soil

Picking out your own soil can be one of the biggest benefits when it comes to growing cannabis. Outside soils are nice, but they don't always have the right nutrients in the right amounts for this kind of plant. When you grow inside, you get to pick out the soil and ensure that it has the right concentration of nutrients for the cannabis, rather than for any other plants. This can give you the peace of mind knowing that your plants are well taken care of.

More convenient for smaller spaces

It is not always possible to grow a garden outside. You may be worried about someone coming in and stealing your plants, especially if you don't have a fence, or you just may live in an area without the space, such as a backyard. Growing your cannabis inside can make it easier to watch out for, doesn't matter how much space you have, and can be really convenient when you are learning the process.

Need to have artificial lights

One thing to remember when you are growing your cannabis plants is that you must have some kind of lighting system. The plants are not going to do well sitting in your basement and never seeing any light. If possible, place the plants in a kind of greenroom or in another room that will give them direct sunlight. When living in an area that is dark or doesn't get a lot of sunlight, consider purchasing some artificial lights. These mimic the sun and can provide the plants with the same nutrition and benefits they would get from the sunlight.

Outdoor Gardening

Outdoor gardening is often one of the easiest forms that you can use. Outside of adding in some nutrients to the soil if it's a little bit dry and watering the plants on occasion, outdoor gardening is pretty simple. You can tend to the garden when it works out the best for you and as long as the plants are getting a bit of care, you will find they produce a good yield. While this method can cause some issues if you don't have a lot of space in the backyard, it can work well for most people.

Get natural sunlight

Nothing is better for your cannabis plants than getting natural sunlight. While it is possible to purchase some lights that can help mimic the sun, none of them are going to work as well as the sunlight can. It provides some extra strength and nutrients to the plants without you having to worry about more on your electricity bill or how long the plants have gotten their light.

When picking out a place to grow these plants, make sure that you are getting enough sunlight. You want to pick out a place that will give at least a few hours of sunlight every day for your plants, has the right amount and type of soil, and will be able to get enough water, or is at least close enough to a water source to make watering easy, to take care of your plants.

Fertile soil

Outdoor gardening of your plants can be nice because you can give them the natural vitamins and nutrients that come from the soil. There are many places in your yard that have these nutrients just waiting to be used. Other times, you may have to put in a little bit of work to get the soil to be just right. Simply adding in a little mulch and some other nutrients can do the trick and you will have endless gardening space that your plants will love.

Rain water

With outdoor planting, you won't have to worry so much about providing the right amount of water to your plants. You will still need to check on them every once in a while, but often Mother Nature will take care of the work for you. Rain water often has more of the nutrients that your plants need to do well and you will just need to check up, rather than constantly water, to make your plants happy.

More space for plants to grow

When you are able to plant the cannabis outside, you are giving them more room to grow. You will have any space outside, rather than a small pot inside the home, and often you won't have to worry about transplanting your plants at all because they are fine in the one location. The cannabis plants will be able to expand their roots and grow strong without having to worry about changing out of pots or other issues.

Picking whether to grow your plants inside or outside can sometimes be up to your personal preferences. Just make sure that you are giving the plants the proper care that they need and you will be amazed at the yield you can get in no time.

Chapter 3: The Basics of Growing Cannabis

Once you have decided whether to grow your cannabis inside your home or outdoors, it is time to get started with growing the plant. This can be a really rewarding experience as long as you get it done right and understand how to pick the right seeds, pick the right soil, and the other details that go into growing your cannabis. In this chapter you will learn all the basics so you are set to go!

Steps to Growing Cannabis

Picking Seeds

The first thing that you will need to do when starting to grow your cannabis is pick out the right seeds. You will need to pick out the kind of strain that you would like to go with including auto-flowering, sativa, and indica strains. All of them will have different benefits that you may enjoy and can provide different potencies.

Often it is up to personal preference, and the end result that you would like, that determines which seeds that you will pick.

The next thing to consider is how much room you will have to grow in. This will determine how many seeds you will be able to purchase because you need to have enough room without the plants competing for nutrients. You should consider the kind of medium that you plan to use with the seeds, such as whether you are using hydroponics or soil, since each of the strains will work differently with these systems. Also consider how long you have in the season, how much yield you would like to get from the seeds, and whether you have the time commitment for each type before beginning.

Germination

Once you have picked out your seeds, it is time to get them growing. You will need to germinate the seeds before planting by simply placing them into a glass of distilled water for 24 hours. After this time has passed, take them out of the water and into a warm and moist paper towel. You should be able to see that the seed has sprouted its taproot and you will be able to place it into the growing medium of your choice.

Seedlings

The next part is going to take a few weeks to accomplish to have a little bit of patients. Over the next two to four weeks, depending on the strain of seeds that you picked, you will start to see that your seed starts to sprout the first true leaves. At this point the seed has changed into a seedling. It will need some special care during this time, including at least sixteen hours of light every day, to help it get the proper care and attention while growing. Be careful with the light being too strong at this point since the marijuana plant is delicate and bright lights can cause damage.

Vegetative Growth

During the next stage, your plant is going to start to develop quite a bit. You will start to see changes that happen almost daily in terms of the shape and the size of the plant. You will still need to keep them under a strict regimen of sunlight, preferably up to eighteen hours each day, to help them grow. During this stage, you will be able to add in the brighter lights since the plants can handle it a bit better.

This particular stage is going to last for between four and five weeks before the flowering will start, but this can vary based on the strain that you picked out, how long you have the seeds under the lights, and other variables. It is also during this stage that you can take clones of your plant and then train it in order to get a bigger yield without having to restart with brand new seeds, but this is something you can try out as you get more experience.

Male or Female Plants

Most growers want to have their cannabis to grow into unfertilized female plants, or Sensimilla, but you can choose to go with whatever kind works for you. You will be able to determine the sex of the plant by using the pre-flowers that will start to develop during the vegetative growth phase. Even at this point, if you see that the seeds are feminized, there are steps that you can take to change the sex of the plants.

For example, if the plant becomes stressed out it can become a hermaphrodite or will grow as a male. You will need to work hard to prevent some of the most common issues with stress on your plants to keep them growing as female including watching the temperature that your plants are growing in and ensuring that you pick the right kind of light.

Flowering

The flowering stage is the one that you have been waiting for; it is the stage where the plant is finally going to start producing the smokable buds which is the main goal of most growers. This is the stage where you will be able to reduce some of the light that your plants are using since most of them will simply need twelve hours of light compared to the other stages. The brightness of the bulb also needs to be lowered to ensure that the plant isn't being damaged. Keep with this regimen until the plants are ready for harvest.

Harvesting

As a beginner, it may be difficult to tell when it is time to harvest your plants, but it is one of the most important steps if you would like to get the most out of these plants. You may need to bring in some helping equipment to make it easier for your eyes to spot the signs for harvesting. One way to tell that the plants are ready is to check their trichomes. You will need a magnifying glass to look and see if 80 percent of the trichomes are cloudy, five percent are clear, and fifteen percent are amber.

While checking, realize that you won't be able to get this right all of the time. You won't have something telling you this, but if the amounts match to being close to these percentages, the plant is ready to be harvested. Get ready to chop the flowers and get ready to dry and cure them for use.

Drying and Curing

At this point, you may be ready to take the flowers and just start smoking those buds right away. But this is not the time to start smoking the buds if you want to get the most enjoyment out of your work. You will find that drying and curing your weed will make it more enjoyable compared to just harvesting the buds and then taking them.

To dry the weed, you will need to hang up the buds and keep them there until they start to feel dry to the touch. You don't want to leave them up there too long, just until you feel they are dry to the touch. After this time, you can use the process called burping which is just placing the buds into a glass jar, Mason jars work well for this, and then leave them inside over the next month. You should open it a few minutes twice a day during this month to allow a bit of air in, but otherwise you can leave alone until you are done with the month.

Once you have gone through the steps above, you will have some of the best cannabis to enjoy. This is one of the best ways to do it, at home, because you know the exact strain that you have, you can save money from a dealer, and you won't have to worry about running out or a bad mix from someone else. Follow these simple steps and see how easy it can be to work on growing your own cannabis.

Simple Tools Needed to Grow Cannabis

Growing your cannabis plants is similar to growing other plants in your garden. The cannabis is going to need some special care and attention to grow big and strong, but with some dedication and good work, you will be able to see some high yields from your hard work. Here are a few of the basic tools that you will need to ensure that your cannabis plants are growing strong and you are getting the results that you want.

Water

Your cannabis is not going to grow strong if it doesn't have a good source of water. You should pick out water that is at a neutral pH and if the water doesn't reach this pH, you may need to alter it a little bit. With the outdoor garden, you may be fine using just the water that comes from your hose as well as rain water. It is possible to use tap water to take care of your plants when growing them indoors, but test the water first to make sure it reaches the right pH to be healthy for your plants.

During the growing process, your plants will need a lot of water. This water is going to carry a lot of nutrients to the roots and ensures that your marijuana is able to grow healthy and strong. Check on your plants often to see if they need more water to grow strong, but be careful to not put too much water into the ground as this can rot the roots.

Light

The light source that you choose will make all the difference in how well your weed will grow. If you have chosen to grow this plant outside, the light source is not as important because you have the sun helping you out. But if you are growing these plants inside, you will need to take special precautions to ensure that the plants get the right kind and right amount of light to grow strong. There are different cycles of lighting that are needed in each stage of your plant growth so consider getting a few different types of lights with different intensities, and even ones that have timers so you ensure the plants are getting just the right amount of light that they need.

Nutrients

You need to make sure that your cannabis is getting the right nutrients to stay healthy. Sometimes this is present in the soil that you pick out, but often you need to add in a helping hand to ensure that the plants are going to do just fine. There is no harm in adding in these nutrients, and often it can result in the best yields compared to those who just leave the soil alone.

You do need to exercise some care when it comes to picking out the right nutrients for your plants. You should make sure that the three main ingredients, potassium, phosphorous, and nitrogen, are present in the soil when growing marijuana. You can get a tester to see how the outdoor soil is doing in the area where you would like to grow the plants. If they are missing out on a key nutrient, consider adding in some mulch or mixing in potting soil with these nutrients.

Things get a bit easier when you use your own soil, such as with indoor gardening. This allows you to pick out the exact soil that you would like to use to keep the plants growing strong. You should check the bag of anything that you plan to use with growing and ensure there are high levels of the three nutrients to help your plants grow.

Chapter 4: Dealing with Pests and Other Gardening Issues

When you are growing your cannabis plants, you will want to make sure that you are giving them the proper care and attention. While there are many issues to consider, such as making sure the plant is growing properly, you are giving the plant the right amount of water and nutrition, and that the plant is getting enough sun, you also need to be on the watch for pests and bugs who may hinder your plant.

No matter what kind of plant you grow, it is possible to see pests and bugs try to take over. They are looking for an easy way to get their dinner and if you don't take the proper precautions, you are going to find that your marijuana plants are starting to fade and it could be too late to give them the help that they need. Whether you are trying to be proactive and keep the pests and bugs at bay or you are already dealing with these common issues, here are some tips to help out when those pests come to town.

Best Control Methods for Pests

There are a number of effective methods that you can use for pest control with your cannabis plants. No matter which one you choose, you need to be on the lookout for pests and start the pest control early for the best results. Some of the methods that you can consider for pest control include:

Predators

Adding in some predators can help to keep those pests away. Options like lacewings, praying mantises, and ladybugs can all be predators to common pests that may affect your plants. You can purchase these commercially and let the free into your garden. You won't have to worry about them taking advantage of your growing plants and they will kill off any of the pests and bugs that have been causing you some issues.

Keep in mind that you need to keep the natural order of things where you are growing. Don't try to introduce new animals to an area they haven't been before. Try to bring in just one or two types of predators to the area and let them do their job. Adding in too many different types of bugs can cause some attention, cause the predators to fight amongst each other, and can even make your plants suffer.

Organic Insecticides

Since you are growing the cannabis to consume, you need to be really careful about the kinds of insecticides that you are using. While these chemicals can do a great job at keeping away those bugs and pests, if you pick out some of the commercial brands, you may have some issues with adding harmful things into your plants and to your health. Going with organic will prevent some of these issues and they work just as well as other options.

Pyrethrum is a good choice to use because it is organic and is considered to have one of the best strengths when it comes to insecticides. It will also work with many different pests so you can use it on anything that is bothering your garden. Remember, even when it comes to organic varieties, you may need to add in some water so read the instructions to ensure you are applying correctly.

While the organic insecticides do not contain some of the chemicals that traditional insecticides do, it can make a big difference on the amount of pests in your garden with all natural materials that are safe for your plants while killing off the pests. If you tried using predators and they are starting to take over your garden as well, your organic insecticides can help out with these as well. Read the ingredients on all of your chosen insecticides have the right chemicals to keep the garden growing strong.

Homemade Remedies

If you are worried about the pests in your garden and don't want to allow harmful chemicals into the cannabis plants, you can choose to make some of your own homemade remedies. These are easy to make and often just include one or two ingredients. These remedies will drive the pests insane, or keep them away in the first place, and you won't have to worry about the quality or taste of your cannabis.

There are a number of options that you can use to help keep your cannabis plants safe. One option is to take two tablespoons of soap and dilute it into a gallon of water. Add this into a spray bottle and mist it onto your plants. Try to apply this as evenly as possible to your plant. Let this mixture set for a few minutes and then spray it with some normal water to get the soap off to prevent damage.

Another option that can be really good for keeping beetles away is to make a mixture of garlic while using some alcohol in soapy water can be good for keeping away the slugs and snails. Mint works well with many pests and can keep your plants safe without any harmful side effects. There are quite a few recipes that you will be able to use on your plants that use a few essential oils and are safe for the plants. Be careful to find the right recipe that will keep your plants healthy without affecting the quality or taste while keeping away all of those nasty pests.

Pests can cause a lot of damage to your plants. They could start to eat up at your cannabis, thinking that it tastes a lot like a great dinner, but making it impossible to get the yield that you are looking for. Using some natural remedies, whether you are making these on your own or getting an organic insecticide, compared to purchasing a commercial insecticide, can help to keep these pests away without the harmful chemicals. Try out a few of these options and see how amazing they work for the health of your plant.

Companion Planting

If you are doing your cannabis growing outside, consider doing companion planting. There are some plants that are grown in the wild and can help to repel pests naturally. If you add in a few of these plants to your cannabis garden, they will keep the pests away without any extra work on your part. Some of the plants that do a great job of this include onions, cabbages, and mints. Any plant that is pretty odorous can help out as well.

These plants can naturally keep away all the pests while also helping to camouflage the growing area you are using for the cannabis. Just remember to plant each of these apart from each other to ensure that the cannabis and the other plants are not competing for nutrients or water in the garden. You may also need to make some changes to the nutrient density in your soil if using companion planting to ensure that both types of plants are getting all of the nutrition that they need and don't start dying out.

Chapter 5: Consider a Hydroponic System

So far in this guidebook, we have been talking about using the traditional method of growing plants, using the soil, to help the plant grow strong. But in some cases, it may be best to use a slightly different method. One of the most successful methods, and a really effective one if you choose to grow your plants inside. You will not need to worry about the soil quality and can add the nutrients right into your water and directly into the plants, rather than worrying about whether the soil is suitable. While it can take some time to set up the hydroponic system, it is the most effective method and can help you to get the most out of your marijuana crop.

What is Hydroponics?

Hydroponics is simply the method of growing your plants, any plants, in a water based solution that is full of nutrients. The process of hydroponics will not use any soil. In most cases, your plant do not need this soil, they simply need to have the nutrients that are found in the soil. The hydroponic system takes out the middle man and just adds the nutrients to the water to give to the plants.

You will need to support the root system in a medium of some kind which can include peat moss, clay pellets, rockwool, or perlite. But most of the work is going to be done with the help of the nutrient rich water. The roots need to stay in contact with the water at all times so that the nutrients will get right into the plant without delay and help it to grow.

The nice part about this is you get the chance to control the nutrients so much easier compared to using the soil. With soil, you can test a bit, but it is not always certain that you know exactly how much of each nutrient is found inside. Adding too much or too little can have an adverse effect on your plants and it is hard to tell until something goes wrong with your cannabis plant. But with the hydroponic system, you get to be in direct control of your nutrient content. You can add in the exact amount that is needed and change the amounts easier if you need during the growing process.

Advantages of Hydroponics

There are many benefits you will be able to enjoy when you choose to use hydroponics for your cannabis plants. The biggest benefit is that you are going to get a much better yield with your plants. The cannabis will be able to grow faster and produce more out of each seed with this kind of system. In fact, if you are able to set up the system properly, you could get the plants to grow twenty five percent faster and get thirty percent more produce compared to the same plant being grown in the soil. This can save you a lot of time and you will always have cannabis ready when you need it.

Another benefit is that you can control the nutrients that go into your plant. Trying to figure out how many nutrients are inside your soil can be hard. There are systems in place that can help you to figure out a rough estimate of the nutrients that are inside, but these are not the most accurate. You could easily add in too much of the nutrients into your soil or have too little, and your plant will be the one to suffer.

When you use a hydroponic system, you will not have to guess. You will know right away how much you have inside the system and can easily add in more or less as you need. Plus, your roots are going to be directly in contact with the nutrients, rather than having to worry about the roots having to go through the soil to get the nutrients. The roots will get the right nutrients when they need it the most and you won't have to worry about washing out the nutrients or any other issues with your plant growing properly.

Disadvantages of a Hydroponics System

While there are quite a few benefits to having this kind of system for your cannabis plants, there are a few things that you will need to keep in mind and which may make it easier to use soil on your plants. The biggest factor to consider is that a hydroponics system is going to cost a bit more compared to just getting soil, but you are able to reuse the hydroponics system so that can help to offset some of the costs.

In addition, if you are using the hydroponics system on a large scale, it can take some time to set up. You may have to do a bit of trial and error to figure out the best way to do your system and to ensure that your plants can get the best nutrition. If you don't have a lot of time to get this all set up, it may be easier to get your plants to grow in the soil.

The biggest risk that can come with a hydroponic system is that a simple issue can kill off the plants pretty quickly. For example, if you have a failure in the pump, your plants may all die off while you are at work. This is because the plants are completely dependent on a water supply that is fresh in this system and if the pump isn't pushing the water through, your plants will not make it.

The hydroponic system can be a great way for you to make sure that you get more yield out of your marijuana. You do need to have a little extra time to take care of this system without ruining any of your plants by something breaking. If you are never home and can't give it the attention that it needs, this probably isn't the best choice for you. On the other hand, if you would like to find a method of growing that helps your cannabis yield more than ever and isn't too difficult to take on, this may be the best growing system you have heard about.

Types of Hydroponic Systems

There are a number of hydroponic systems that you can choose from. Each one will need slightly different materials and will work differently, but they all work on the same system and can help you to get some of the best results out of your cannabis production. Some of the options that you can choose with your hydroponic systems include:

Deepwater Culture

This method of hydroponics is also known as the reservoir method. It is one of the easiest methods to do and therefor great for beginners who have never done hydroponics. In this method, the roots of the plant are going to be suspended into the nutrient solution. You will then need an air pump to oxygenate the nutrient solution so that the roots will not drown. You will need to take care to not allow sunlight to get into the system since this can cause a lot of algae to grow and make the system worthless.

The biggest benefit of using this method is that you will not have to worry about the spray or drip emitters clogging up. This can keep the water flowing easily as long as the pump is working properly and can even help out if you want to use the system for organic growing compared to some of the other options.

Nutrient Film Technique

Next on the list of systems to try is the Nutrient Film Technique. This is a hydroponic system where the nutrients are going to flow right over the roots of your plant. The system will be set up on a slight tilt so that the nutrients are going to flow thanks to gravity. This will require less work to use and can ensure that your roots are getting all the nutrients that they need through the day.

The NFT technique works well because the roots will be able to absorb more of the oxygen that is in the air around them compared to what they can get right out of the nutrient solution. With this method, the roots will just touch the nutrient solution with their tipis so the plant will be able to utilize the oxygen in the air to get a faster rate of growth.

Aeroponics

In this option, the roots of your cannabis plants will be misted with the nutrient solution while they are suspended in the air. There are two methods used with this in order to ensure that the roots are getting their nutrients. The first one is to use a spray bottle or other spray nozzle source to mist the solution onto the roots. The other one is known as a pond fogger that will require a bit more work but can take care of the misting process for you.

Wicking

This is another easy method of hydroponics that also won't cost you a lot of extra money. The concept with this option is that you will use a material, sometimes cotton works well, to surround the growing medium with the edge in the nutrient solution. This will bring the nutrient solution back to the roots of your plant so it stays strong. You can choose to use a medium, such as vermiculite, to do this rather than adding in a wicking material to make things easier.

Ebb and Flow

The ebb and flow system is good for helping to keep the good nutrients going towards the plant. This system is going to flood the area where you are growing your plants with the nutrient solution at intervals that you have set up. The nutrient solution will stay there for a bit, but slowly starts to drain back into the reservoir that you set up. You will need to set up a pump and place it onto a timer so that the plants are consistently getting the nutrients that it needs throughout the day. This system is often used for plants that need to go through short periods of being dry and can help the roots grow stronger as they search for more water.

Each of these hydroponic systems can be a great addition to your growing process. The important thing to remember is to pick one that works in your space and fits your time and budget concerns. In addition, you will need to be careful about changing out the nutrient solution on occasion. Do not get lazy and just feed the plants the same solution; you should be changing out the solution once ever few weeks at maximum because the plants will start to lose the nutrients over time.

Chapter 6: Troubleshooting Issues With Your Cannabis

When you first get started with growing your marijuana plants, you may be worried about getting them to grow in the proper manner. There are a lot of things that can go wrong when you start growing these plants, but having the right knowledge in place and taking it one step at a time can ensure that those plants are going to look amazing at the end. Here are some of the most common problems that you can have with your marijuana plants and some of the best tips for how to help them out.

Seeds

First, let's take a look at the seeds. This is the first thing that you will get before growing and if you don't take good care of the seeds, it is going to be almost impossible to get a good crop out of them. Some of the most common types of issues that come with the seeds include:

- White or brittle seed—if you put a light pressure onto the seeds and they crush, these seeds are not going to germinate or do well. You should pick out another type of seed to start with.
- Green seed—this is not really an issue with your seed, it just shows that the seed is immature. As the seed starts to ripen, it is going to get darker. Once it is a darker color, go ahead and plant it.
- Small seed—it is always best to go with the largest seed that you can find. Of course, there are some plants that produce smaller seeds and these work fine, but the bigger ones will last longer and do a better job with producing the best buds.

Roots

The roots of your cannabis need to be strong and secure since these provide a lot of the nutrients that your plants need to thrive. You may have to look for other issues in the plant to determine that something is wrong with the root since you are not able to see this part of the plant. Some of the common issues that come with the roots include:

- Tight packed roots—a symptom of this is roots that are not growing properly because the roots don't have room. You will need to transplant the cannabis so that the roots can grow more as well as the plant. If the roots are already in a small ball from growing in a tiny container, you may need to massage them a bit to loosen up the area.
- Sparse roots—the solution to this problem will vary depending on the stage of growth you are in. but in most cases, this problem is going to occur if you are not maintaining the right pH levels or providing enough oxygen to the roots. The drainage in the soil can be bad or you should add in some more air stone to the hydroponic system.

- Slimy and smelly roots—this is another issue that can come about with lack of oxygen. When the oxygen is missing, you will end up with the issue of root rot, which can be smelly and difficult. While it is possible to save the roots, you are not going to get that much for the yield and your results will not be that impressive. Keep this as a learning experience and avoid the issues later.

Stems

As your plant starts to grow, you will want to watch out for the health of the stems. This is the trunk of your plant and each stem is really important to ensuring that the flower is growing properly and gets all of the nutrients that it needs. Keep in mind with your stems that since they are composed mostly of water to carry the nutrients, they are going to be pretty light once they are dried out. Some of the most common issues that can occur with the stems of your cannabis include:

- Leaning branches—sometimes the flowers can start to weigh too much and cause the branches and the stem to lean over a bit. The best thing to do for this is to tie up the branches. You can also turn on a fan inside to help stimulate the motions of the wind, which can sometimes cause the stems to strengthen up.

- Thin and spindly stalks—this issue occurs often when there is not enough light for the plant to grow. If they aren't near enough to the light source, move them closer, change the kind of light that you are using, or have the light on the plant for a longer period of time through the day. Sometimes a weak root system can cause this problem as well so consider that when making changes.

- Broken stems—when you first get started, you may be really worried when the stem breaks. The most likely cause of a broken stem is because the grower is messing around with the plant and trying to get it to bend or move too roughly. Luckily, simply taping the stem back together and adding in a bit of support can help the plant to heal from the issues.

You will notice a knot where the break occurred, but after the stem heals, it will keep growing just fine.

Leaves

The leaves are an important part of your growing plant and they need to get the proper care to grow big and strong. The leaves are the part of the plant that absorb the light and uses it in the process of photosynthesis. They are kind of like the lungs and sensory organs of the plants. They are also one of the first parts that will show a sign when something is going wrong. Unfortunately, even after fixing the issue, the leaves often won't recover, but you will see new leaves that come in their place and show that you are doing the work properly. Some of the most common issues with leaves in your plant include:

- Drooping leaves—over and under watering your plant can cause the dropping leaves. When using soil, you should wait until the soil starts to dry up a bit to the touch before watering again. For hydroponic systems, consider adding in some more oxygen to the roots to help out.

- Leaves with the edges curled down (broad leaves)—this is an issue that comes up when the humidity gest too high. It won't cause harm to your plant, but it can make the harvest less than satisfactory.
- Leaves with the edges curled up (narrow leaves)—this problem will show that humidity is low in the area. It does not cause harm, but you may want to consider adding in some humidity to get the best results.
- Yellowing of the leaves—often this shows that the plants are deficient in nitrogen. If there are some browning on the leaf tips, you are over fertilizing the plants. You may need to flush the plant with some extra water to help remove some of these extra nutrients and keep it growing strong. If this doesn't work, add in a bit more nitrogen to the soil or check to see how the pH is doing.
- Brown or purple spots on a stunted plant—this is a sign that your plants are not getting the best amount of phosphorus.

Check to see if the pH balance is on for your plants and consider adding in a bit more phosphorus to the water to help out.

- Pale, brown, and tan spots on the leaves—this is another sign of a phosphorus deficiency and can also show that the plants have come in contact with a pest.
- Yellowing between the veins of the leaf—this shows that the plant is not getting enough potassium. Add in a bit more to your water and check to see if the pH is balancing out again.
- Leaves turn white or pale yellow in the veins—this is a sign that the iron is low in your plant and it will soon stop growing properly. Add in some more trace nutrients or chelated iron and your pH balance will get back on track.

Flowers

You will need to take some time on the flowers if you want to get the best buds from your hard work. The flowers are the only part that contain the compounds that can get the user high and without taking care of any potential issues that could come to the flowers. Some of the most common problems that can come with the flowers of your cannabis and how you can work to make them better:

- The flowers are stunted and have bumps between the pistils—this means that the plant has become pollinated. The bumps that you are seeing are simply seeds.
- Internode spacing is wider with airy buds—this happens when the temperatures change quite a bit in between the day and the night. While this can be a hard thing to control when planting outside, when growing inside, you can adjust the lights to keep the temperature pretty steady.
- Powdery coating on the buds—this is different compared to the trichomes crystals that coat the flowers. This kind of coating is going to look web like and whispy and could be a type of mold or a pest. No matter what it is, it is causing issues with how your plant is growing. You can look at the pest section if you think this is the issue or use a neem oil to

help get rid of the mold. Make sure to not eat the moldy bud since this can make you really sick.

- Small buds—the buds can help to show how well the plant is growing and developing. Small buds means that you need to add more nutrition to the plant including CO2 during the flowering and lots of ventilation. Control the temperatures and take time to prune your pants so that it can continue growing.

- Buds aren't sticky—this just means that your flowers aren't ready to harvest yet. Allow them to continue growing for a bit longer. It takes at least eight weeks for the finishing strain to finish and other strains can take twelve weeks. You need to give them the right amount of time and you will love the results.

Harvested Flowers

Don't make the mistake of thinking that once you harvest the flowers you are done with the work. There are other issues that can occur with the flowers, even after you have harvested them. You will need to treat and pay attention to the buds once you take them from the plant. Some issues to watch out for when you are done with harvesting the buds include:

- Crispy and crumbly buds—you most likely allowed the buds to dry out too much, and often the drying out process went too quickly. Be careful next time to go a bit slower.
- Pliable stems with the bud still dry—this means that there is still some more moisture inside the buds.
- Powdery tendrils on the flowers—this is mildew and mold. You will need to allow the buds to get a bit more air. It is possible to post process the moldy buds with extracts such as water hashes, though you will need to do a generous amount of freezing first.
- Buds have a smell and taste like hay—this is a characteristic of immature buds. A slow and long cure can help to solve this issue.

- Buds burn to a black ash—this happens when there is too much phosphorus left during the flowering process of the plant. A long cure that is slow and dry can help with this process. You will just need to be sure to do a good flush before harvesting the next time.
- Harsh smoke—this could possibly occur from over fertilizing. The proper curing and drying will help to give a smooth smoke even when you over fertilize.

During the first few sessions of growing cannabis, you will find that some of these mistakes are pretty easy to make. Over time, you will learn how to handle these common issues a bit better and can take the proper steps to avoid having something go wrong with your harvest. Take your time, learn some of the signs to watch out for, and soon you will be able to grow the perfect crop each and every time.

Conclusion

Growing cannabis in your home does not have to be a big challenge. Even if you have never gotten started with growing in the past, whether with cannabis or with other plants in your garden, you will find that growing cannabis can be pretty easy to handle. With a little bit of care and ensuring that you are catching any of the issues that come up with the plant, you could get the exact strain of cannabis that you want without having to rely on any alternate sources.

When you are ready to get started with growing your own cannabis, no matter whether you would like to do it inside or outside or you have just started, you will find all the information that you need inside this guidebook!